modern readers · stage 1

Fire in the Forest

Eduardo Amos
Elisabeth Prescher
Ernesto Pasqualin

2nd edition

© EDUARDO AMOS, ELISABETH PRESCHER, ERNESTO PASQUALIN, 2005

Richmond

Diretoria: *Paul Berry*
Gerência editorial: *Sandra Possas*
Coordenação de revisão: *Estevam Vieira Lédo Jr.*
Coordenação de produção gráfica: *André Monteiro, Maria de Lourdes Rodrigues*
Coordenação de produção industrial: *Wilson Troque*

Projeto editorial: *Kylie Mackin*

Edição e preparação de texto: *Kylie Mackin*
Assistência editorial: *Gabriela Peixoto Vilanova*
Revisão: *Maria Cecília Kinker Caliendo*
Projeto gráfico de miolo e capa: *Ricardo Van Steen Comunicações e Propaganda Ltda./Oliver Fuchs*
Edição de arte: *Christiane Borin*
Ilustrações de miolo e capa: *Rogério Borges*
Diagramação: *Formato Comunicação*
Pré-impressão: *Helio P. de Souza Filho, Marcio H. Kamoto*
Impressão e acabamento: *Gráfica Printi*
Lote: *799488*
Código: *12040950*

Dados Internacionais de Catalogação na Publicação (CIP)
(Câmara Brasileira do Livro, SP, Brasil)

> Amos, Eduardo
>   Fire in the forest / Eduardo Amos, Elisabeth Prescher, Ernesto Pasqualin. — 2. ed. — São Paulo : Moderna, 2004. — (Modern readers ; stage 1)
>
>   1. Inglês (Ensino fundamental) I. Prescher, Elisabeth. II. Pasqualin, Ernesto. III. Título. IV. Série.
>
> 04-0909   CDD-372.652

Índices para catálogo sistemático:
1. Inglês : Ensino fundamental   372.652

ISBN 85-16-04095-X

Reprodução proibida. Art. 184 do Código Penal e Lei 9.610 de 19 de fevereiro de 1998.

Todos os direitos reservados.

RICHMOND
SANTILLANA EDUCAÇÃO LTDA.
Rua Padre Adelino, 758, 3º andar — Belenzinho
São Paulo — SP — Brasil — CEP 03303-904
www.richmond.com.br
2024

Impresso no Brasil

Chapter 1

Mrs Clapman – Hello.

Mrs Dale – Hello, Mrs Clapman? This is Mrs Dale, Clyde's mother.

Mrs Clapman – How are you, Mrs Dale?

Mrs Dale – I am a little worried. Tomorrow is Clyde's first trip with the scouts. And he is only a cub. Is Ted on the trip, too?

Mrs Clapman – Oh, yes! It is Ted's sixth trip to Hawk Mountain. Don't worry. The camp is very safe.

Mrs Dale – Thanks a lot, Mrs Clapman.

Mrs Clapman – See you tomorrow. Be there at seven o'clock sharp.

The bus is in front of Tiger Cave, the scouts' club. It is almost seven o'clock. The tents, backpacks, sleeping bags, and boxes of food are in the luggage compartment.

Mrs Dale – Clyde is excited about this trip.
Mrs Clapman – All the kids are. This is a real adventure for them!
Mrs Dale – Is it a long trip?

Mrs Clapman – No. Only three hours from here. It's springtime now. The ride is lovely on a warm day. There are lots of flowers and birds in the countryside. The troop leader, Captain Jones, is very experienced. The kids are safe with him.

Chapter 2

After a three-hour trip, the boys are at the camp. At one o'clock, Captain Jones is talking to them.

Captain Jones – Good afternoon, cubs and scouts! Welcome to our camp on Hawk Mountain. This is a special place; it's a nature reserve. Our camp is in the middle of the forest. There are many species of trees and animals here. Our mission is to protect nature. And now, the camp rules…

CAMP RULES
NO FIRES OUTSIDE THE CAMP AREA
NO HUNTING
NO FISHING
NO LITTERING
PRESERVE NATURE
PROTECT WILDLIFE

In the evening, the cubs and scouts are around the campfire. They are all tired but interested in Captain Jones's stories. Captain Jones is an adventurer and a great traveler. His stories are full of danger and mystery.

After a lot of exciting stories, it is bedtime.

Captain Jones – Sorry, boys, bedtime now. Cubs first, then scouts. There are many things to do tomorrow. See you at seven o'clock in the morning. Good night.

Chapter 3

Clyde's Report
Second day at Hawk Mountain C
7:00 a.m. — shower and breakfast
8:00 a.m. — Cubs: clean up the tents the camp area; put water in the tan Scouts: Inspect the forest; make a fir in the evening
10:00 a.m. — swim in the stream
11:00 a.m. — kitchen work
12:00 a.m. — lunch and dishwashing
2:00 p.m. — rest
3:00 p.m. — survival classes in the forest
5:00 p.m. — kitchen work
6:00 p.m. — dinner and dishwashing
7:00 p.m. — talk and songs around the fire
9:00 p.m. — bedtime for cubs
10:00 p.m. — bedtime for scouts

My friend, Ted Clapman, is a scout; he is not homesick. I am a little homesick.

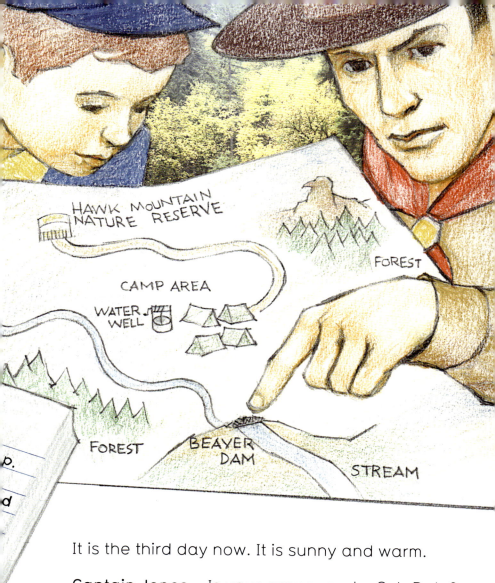

It is the third day now. It is sunny and warm.

Captain Jones – Is your group ready, Cub Dale?
Cub Dale – Yes, sir. What is our task this morning?
Captain Jones – Forest inspection in the stream area.
Cub Dale – Where is the stream, sir?
Captain Jones – Here. Look at the map.

At 10.30, Clyde and his group are by the stream on the top of the hill. The view is beautiful. But... everything is very, very quiet.

Cub Dale – Where are the beavers?... And the birds?

Cub Scott – What's that?
Cub Dale – Where?
Cub Scott – There! Down the hill!
Cub Spencer – Look, there is a lot of smoke.
Cub Dale – And flames, too! Let's call Captain Jones!

There is a fire down the hill and tension in the camp. All the cubs and scouts are around Captain Jones.

Captain Jones – Is everybody here?
Scout Clapman – Yes, sir.
Scout Flanegan – What's the plan, sir?
Captain Jones – Cubs, bring water from the well. Scouts, isolate the fire.
Scout Clapman – Look, Captain. The fire is closer!

Captain Jones – Hurry up, kids! Hurry up!

Clyde and the other cubs bring pails of water from the well. They are very tired. The scouts are very tired, too. The fire is big now.

Scout Clapman – It's impossible, Captain! The fire is out of control!
Cub Dale – Let's call the forest rangers!
Scout Clapman – But they are very far from here.
Captain Jones – Dasher is our only chance. That dog is a fast runner.

Chapter 4

Everybody is very worried at the camp. The fire is too close to the forest.

There are many spots of fire on the hill and a lot of smoke. The cubs are tired and afraid.

Scout Clapman – What now, Captain?
Captain Jones – We are in serious trouble, kids. There isn't enough water here.

Cub Dale – What about the stream, Captain?
Captain Jones – The stream?
Cub Dale – The stream is at the top of the hill. There is a lot of water there!
Captain Jones – That's right, Dale. Great idea! Okay, boys. Everybody to the stream. Hurry up!

Captain Jones and the kids go to the top of the hill.

Scout Clapman – Everybody is here, sir.
Captain Jones – Well, the fire is too big down there, and too close to the forest.
Scout Clapman – What's the plan, sir?

Captain Jones – Look here, kids. This is a beaver dam. There is wood blocking the stream, right?
Cubs and Scouts – Right, sir.
Captain Jones – Let's remove the wood. The water from the stream can extinguish the fire down the hill.
Scout Clapman – Great idea, Captain.
Captain Jones – Then let's go! Cubs to the right with me. Scouts to the left. Hurry!

Boy scouts are well trained. Ten minutes later, there is a loud noise on Hawk Mountain.

There is water running down the hill now. Some minutes later, there is water in the forest. Everyone is very tired. But the forest is safe.

Dasher is back with the forest rangers. The rangers are surprised at the boys' work.

A week later, Captain Jones and the kids are back at Tiger Cave. Everyone is very happy and excited. There is a big celebration.

Captain Jones – You are heroes, kids! There are medals for everyone.
Cub Dale – Hurrah for the Captain!
Everybody – Hurrah!
Captain Jones – And now, the best news: there are no more cubs here. You're all scouts now.

KEY WORDS

The meaning of each word corresponds to its use in the context of the story (see page number 00)

adventure (4) aventura
afraid (14) com medo
after (6) depois
around (7) em volta, ao redor
beaver (10) esquilo
bedtime (7) hora de dormir
bring (12) trazer
camp (3) acampamento
celebration (19) comemoração
closer (12) mais próximo
countryside (5) interior
cub (3) lobinho
dam (17) represa
danger (7) perigo
dishwashing (8) lavagem dos pratos
enough (14) suficiente
excited (4) entusiasmado
experienced (5) experiente
extinguish (17) apagar
fire (6) fogueira
fishing (6) pesca
flame (11) chama
food (4) comida
forest (6) floresta
forest ranger (13) guarda florestal
hero, heroes (19) herói(s)
hill (10) colina, pequena montanha

hunting (6) caça
inspect (8) inspecionar
isolate (12) isolar
leader (5) líder
littering (6) jogar lixo
long (4) longa
loud (17) alto
lovely (5) adorável
luggage compartment (4) bagageiro
medal (19) medalha
mission (6) missão
nature reserve (6) reserva natural
noise (17) barulho
pail (13) balde
place (6) lugar
quiet (10) calmo, quieto
ready (9) pronto
ride (5) passeio
rule (6) regra
runner (13) corredor
safe (3) seguro
scout (3) escoteiro
sharp (3) em ponto
sixth (3) sexto(a)
sleeping bag (4) saco de dormir
smoke (11) fumaça
spot of fire (14) foco de incêndio

springtime (5) primavera
stream (8) riacho
sunny (9) ensolarado
surprised (18) surpreso
survival (8) sobrevivência
task (9) tarefa
tension (12) tensão
tent (4) barraca
then (7) depois
tired (7) cansado
trained (17) treinado
traveler (7) viajante
trip (3) viagem
troop (5) tropa
warm (5) quente

well (12) poço
wildlife (6) vida selvagem
wood (17) madeira
worried (3) preocupado(a)

Expressions

clean up (8) arrumar, limpar
Hurrah! (19) Viva!
Hurry up! (13) Apressem-se!
in trouble (14) em apuros
out of control (13) fora de controle
running down (18) descendo
That's right. (15) É isso mesmo.

ACTIVITIES

Before Reading

1. What is the most famous forest in your country?
2. What are the things you can do in a forest? What are the things you cannot do?

While Reading

Chapter 1

1. Put the sentences in the correct order to form a telephone conversation.
   a) (   ) How are you, Mrs Dale?
   b) (   ) Thanks a lot, Mrs Clapman.
   c) (1) Hello.
   d) (   ) Fine, thanks. I am a little worried.
   e) (   ) See you tomorrow.
   f) (   ) Hello, Mrs Clapman? This is Mrs Dale, Clyde's mother.
   g) (   ) Don't worry. The camp is very safe.

2. Answer T (True), F (False) or D (I don't know).
   a) (   ) It is seven o'clock in the evening.
   b) (   ) All the boys are carrying backpacks.
   c) (   ) The luggage compartment is in the bus.
   d) (   ) Clyde is very excited about the trip.
   e) (   ) It is a long trip.
   f) (   ) The day is humid.
   g) (   ) Captain Jones is a scout.

Chapter 2

3. Unscramble the words to make sentences.
   a) camp / the / forest / in / middle / our / of / is / the

   _____

b) protect / mission / to / our / nature / is
_____

c) Jones / an / and / adventurer / Captain/ great / a / is / traveler
_____

d) o'clock / at / you / seven / in / morning / see / the
_____

4. Write YES for the things you can do in the forest and NO for the things you cannot do.

   _____ fires outside the camp area
   _____ hunting
   _____ fishing
   _____ littering
   _____ preserve nature
   _____ protect wildlife

Chapter 3

5. Check the tasks Clyde had on the second day of the trip.

   _____ do the ironing
   _____ clean up the tents
   _____ make a fire
   _____ put water in the tanks
   _____ watch TV
   _____ wash the dishes
   _____ pack the bags
   _____ clean up camp area
   _____ inspect forest

6. Circle the correct answer.
   1) Cub Dale's group is going to:
      a) inspect the forest   b) inspect the fire
   2) The stream is:
      a) in the mountains   b) on the top of a hill
   3) The view is:
      a) beautiful   b) pretty

4) There is a fire:
   a) down the hill   b) in the camp
5) The forest rangers are:
   a) close   b) far
6) Dasher is a:
   a) dog   b) scout

Chapter 4

7. Read the sentences and write C for Captain Jones, D for Cub Dale and S for Scout Clapman.
   a) ( ) "The stream?"
   b) ( ) "Everybody is here, sir."
   c) ( ) "What about the stream, Captain?"
   d) ( ) "What's the plan, sir?"
   e) ( ) "What now, Captain?"
   f) ( ) "That's right, Dale. Great idea!"
   g) ( ) "Let's remove the wood."

8. Complete the sentences with the words below.

> heroes safe scouts celebration surprised water

   a) There is _____ in the forest.
   b) The rangers are _____ at the boy's work.
   c) The forest is _____.
   d) There is a big _____ at Tiger Cave.
   e) "You are _____, kids!"
   f) "You're all _____ now."

After Reading (Optional Activities)

9. Why do you think there are fires in forests?
10. Nowadays, the forests are disappearing. What can you do to help to protect them?
11. Group work: prepare a poster with pictures or drawings and the title "Let's save the forests!"

Fire in the Forest

"Adventure and human interest for teenagers"

Clyde is excited. It is his first camping trip to the forest with his scout group. He is having a great time with the other kids and learning about environmental conservation. But something is wrong. There are spots of fire down the hill and the forest is in danger. Can the kids help save the forest in time?

Main theme — a fire in a forest area
Other themes — the environment, ethics, solidarity

Visit **www.richmond.com.br** Área exclusiva do professor

stage 4 _ intermediate
stage 3 _ lower intermediate
stage 2 _ elementary
stage 1 _ starter   fiction

STAGE 1

ISBN 85-16-04095-X

modern readers

The Big River

Vera Abi Saber

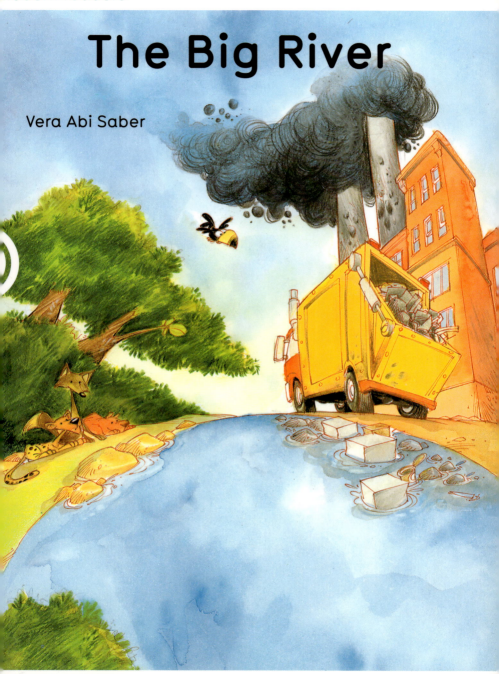

Richmond